Published by Angelis Publications
ISBN: 978-0-9956516-7-8
www.angelispublications.com
Cover Design & Original Artwork: Angie J Anderson

A Celebration of the Life of

*"Life is eternal, and love
is immortal, and death is
only an horizon, and an
horizon is nothing save
the limit of our sight."*

William Penn

Name

Thoughts & Memories

Name

Thoughts & Memories

Name

Thoughts & Memories

Name

Thoughts & Memories

Name Thoughts & Memories

Name | Thoughts & Memories

Name	Thoughts & Memories

Name

Thoughts & Memories

Name

Thoughts & Memories

Name	Thoughts & Memories

Name

Thoughts & Memories

Name

Thoughts & Memories

Name

Thoughts & Memories

Name

Thoughts & Memories

Name

Thoughts & Memories

Name

Thoughts & Memories

Name | Thoughts & Memories

Name

Thoughts & Memories

Name

Thoughts & Memories

Name

Thoughts & Memories

Name

Thoughts & Memories

Name

Thoughts & Memories

Name	Thoughts & Memories

Name | Thoughts & Memories

Name

Thoughts & Memories

Name

Thoughts & Memories

Name | Thoughts & Memories

Name

Thoughts & Memories

Name

Thoughts & Memories

Name

Thoughts & Memories

Name

Thoughts & Memories

Name

Thoughts & Memories

Name

Thoughts & Memories

Name

Thoughts & Memories

Name

Thoughts & Memories

Name

Thoughts & Memories

Name

Thoughts & Memories

Name

Thoughts & Memories

Name

Thoughts & Memories

Name

Thoughts & Memories

Name

Thoughts & Memories

Name

Thoughts & Memories

Name

Thoughts & Memories

Name | Thoughts & Memories

Name

Thoughts & Memories

Name

Thoughts & Memories

Name

Thoughts & Memories

Name

Thoughts & Memories

Name

Thoughts & Memories

Name

Thoughts & Memories

Name | Thoughts & Memories

Name

Thoughts & Memories

Name

Thoughts & Memories

Name

Thoughts & Memories

Name	Thoughts & Memories

Name

Thoughts & Memories

Name | Thoughts & Memories

Name

Thoughts & Memories

Name

Thoughts & Memories

Name

Thoughts & Memories

Name

Thoughts & Memories

Name

Thoughts & Memories

Name | Thoughts & Memories

Name	Thoughts & Memories

Name

Thoughts & Memories

Name

Thoughts & Memories

Name

Thoughts & Memories

Name

Thoughts & Memories

Name

Thoughts & Memories

Name

Thoughts & Memories

Name

Thoughts & Memories

Name

Thoughts & Memories

Name	Thoughts & Memories

Name | Thoughts & Memories

Name | Thoughts & Memories

Name

Thoughts & Memories

Name	Thoughts & Memories

Name

Thoughts & Memories

Name

Thoughts & Memories

Name

Thoughts & Memories

Name

Thoughts & Memories

Name | Thoughts & Memories

Name

Thoughts & Memories

Name

Thoughts & Memories

Name

Thoughts & Memories

Name

Thoughts & Memories

Name

Thoughts & Memories

Name

Thoughts & Memories

Name

Thoughts & Memories

Name

Thoughts & Memories

Name

Thoughts & Memories

Name

Thoughts & Memories

Name

Thoughts & Memories

Name	Thoughts & Memories

www.ingramcontent.com/pod-product-compliance
Lightning Source LLC
Chambersburg PA
CBHW080810020826
48982CB00018B/986

* 9 7 8 0 9 9 5 6 5 1 6 7 8 *